Introduction

Whether you're preparing Chuckie's Upchuck for a potluck supper, Phlegm Brûlée for a festive party, or Pus Pockets as a quick after-school snack, the recipes in *Creepy Cuisine* are designed to unleash the grisly gourmet *buried* in everyone. But before you get cooking, here are some tips to help you survive in the kitchen.

Scared Safe!

1. Always ask an adult for permission before cooking any recipe.

2. Always have an adult help you use the oven and stove.

3. Always ask an adult to help you use knives, vegetable peelers, graters, scissors, and electrical appliances.

4. Always wash your hands with soap and water before preparing food.

5. Wear an apron or smock to protect your clothes while cooking.

6. When cooking on the stove, always turn pot handles away from you so you won't knock over pots by accident.

7. Always turn off burners before removing pots or pans from the stove.

8. Use thick pot holders or wear oven mitts whenever you're removing a pot or pan from the oven (or whenever you're handling any hot pot or pan).

9. Ask an adult for help when draining hot foods through a colander.

10. Make sure your hands are dry when handling electrical appliances.

11. Wipe up all spills immediately (so you don't fall on a slippery floor!).

12. Roll up your sleeves, and keep dish towels and pot holders away from a hot stove so they don't catch fire. Always have a fire extinguisher in your kitchen, and know how to use it!

Terms of Torture

beat - to mix in a steady motion by hand or with an electric mixer

boil - to cook until bubbles rise and break on the surface of a liquid

chop - to cut into small pieces

colander - a bowl with many holes used to drain water from spaghetti, vegetables, and other foods

cube or **dice** - to cut into tiny squares, all of the same size

double boiler - a large pot partially filled with simmering water, with a smaller pot sitting partway inside the larger pot (cooking takes place inside the smaller pot)

dust - to coat lightly with flour or sugar

grease or **butter** - to rub oil or butter on the inside surface of a pan

mash - to reduce to a smooth consistency

mince - to chop into fine pieces

mix - to stir ingredients together with a spoon

peel or **pare** - to remove skin from a vegetable or fruit

preheat - to allow oven to heat to the appropriate cooking temperature before food is put inside

sauté - to fry quickly in a small amount of oil until lightly browned and tender

simmer - to cook below boiling over a low heat (only a few bubbles appear on the surface of the liquid)

toss - to mix ingredients gently

whip - to beat rapidly

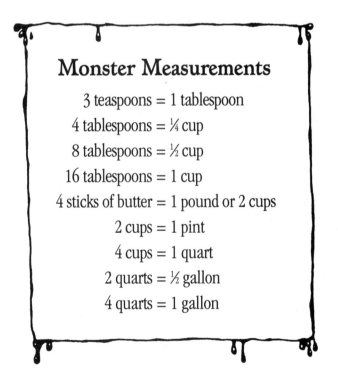

Monster Measurements

3 teaspoons = 1 tablespoon

4 tablespoons = ¼ cup

8 tablespoons = ½ cup

16 tablespoons = 1 cup

4 sticks of butter = 1 pound or 2 cups

2 cups = 1 pint

4 cups = 1 quart

2 quarts = ½ gallon

4 quarts = 1 gallon

Covering Your Tracks

1. As you finish using utensils, pots, and pans, soak them in hot, soapy water. (If you are going to wash utensils, pots, or pans in a dishwasher, scrape the food particles off them and rinse with water before loading the machine.)

2. Wash knives separately, holding the handle of the knife, not the blade!

3. When you are done cooking, always check the oven and stove to make sure they're shut off.

4. Wash and dry all counters and cooking surfaces when you've finished cooking. (Make sure the cooking surfaces have cooled down first!)

5. Check the floor for spills and crumbs, and wipe them up.

6. Unplug all appliances and put them away.

7. Make sure leftovers are securely covered, dated, and stored away.

Horror
d'Oeuvres

Gory Gorilla Tonsils

Think you *have a sore throat?*

2 dozen Brussels sprouts
¼ teaspoon salt
1 cup grated American cheese (¼ pound)
2 tablespoons milk
10-12 iceberg lettuce leaves, washed and dried
¼ teaspoon paprika

What You'll Need
sharp knife • large pot • fork • colander • small saucepan
• wooden spoon • large platter

1. Wash the Brussels sprouts and remove any discolored leaves. Trim off the stem ends and, with an adult's help, cut an X into the bottom of each sprout to make sure your tonsils cook nice and tender.

2. Place the sprouts in a pot containing about 2 inches of water and sprinkle with the salt. Cover the pot and, with an adult's help, cook over medium heat until boiling. After 8 to 10 minutes, carefully stab a few sprouts with a fork to see if they're tender. When you can easily pierce them through to their centers, remove the pot from the heat and carefully drain the sprouts in a colander.

3. Place the grated cheese in a small saucepan and add the milk. With an adult's help, simmer over low heat, stirring continuously with a wooden spoon until the cheese melts. Remove the saucepan from the heat as soon as the cheese is melted.

10

4. Arrange a bed of washed lettuce leaves on a platter. Place the gorilla tonsils—in pairs, of course—on the leaves. Drizzle the melted cheese (pus) over the tonsils. Sprinkle with paprika (blood specks) and serve.

Serves 6 little surgeons.

Serving Idea

Make yourself a surgical mask to wear while serving this dish! Put a string through opposite sides of a gauze pad and tie the gauze around your head, covering your mouth. (And serve ice cream for dessert out of respect for your tonsil-less gorilla's giant sore throat!)

11

Crudités with Vomit Vinaigrette

You'll turn heads and *stomachs with this deliciously disgusting dip!*

cherry tomatoes	mushroom caps
bunch of carrots, peeled	2 cups cottage cheese (1 pound)
or scraped	1 envelope dry onion soup mix
zucchini	¼ cup milk
celery stalks	yellow food coloring
radishes	

What You'll Need
paper towel • vegetable peeler • sharp knife • mixing spoon • small bowl • serving platter

1. Before you begin your vomit sauce, you have to prepare your raw vegetables, or "crudités." (Use whatever quantity and selection of raw vegetables you think your guests would enjoy. Allow approximately 1 heaping handful per person.)

2. First rinse all the vegetables in warm water except the mushroom caps (wipe those gently with a damp paper towel). Then, with an adult's help, carefully slice the carrots, zucchini, and celery into thin sticks. The cherry tomatoes can be served whole, but you may want to remove any green stems. The radishes and mushrooms can be halved or served whole. If you are not serving this dish right away, put the vegetables in a plastic bag and store them in the refrigerator to keep them fresh and crispy.

3. In a small bowl, mix the cottage cheese, the onion soup mix, and the milk. Stir in some food coloring until you get the desired yellowish color. Do not overmix. Lumpy is more realistic!

4. Now arrange your vegetables on a platter surrounding the Vomit Vinaigrette. Smack your lips and dip!

Serves 6 to 8 strong-stomached guests.

Serving Idea

Vomit Vinaigrette tastes great in sandwiches, too! Try splattering some into pita pockets!

Rotting Crone's Kisses

When you open wide, don't let your teeth fall out!

½ pound fresh peas in the pod
green food coloring
8 ounces cream cheese, softened
6-12 large round crackers (approximately 3 x 3 inches)
1 (6-ounce) jar pimientos, drained
1 cup raisins

What You'll Need
2 small bowls • mixing spoon
• dull knife • scissors • serving platter

1. Open the pea pods and remove the peas into a bowl. Set peas aside.

2. In another small bowl, mix food coloring, drop by drop, into the cream cheese, stirring with a spoon until the desired shade of green is reached.

3. Spread a large thin oval of cream cheese on each cracker.

4. With an adult's help, use clean scissors to cut pimientos into upper and lower lip shapes. (You'll need 1 upper and 1 lower lip for each cracker.) Using extra cream cheese, if necessary, to adhere lips to crackers, place a set of lips on top of each cracker, surrounding the oval of cream cheese. This will form your open mouth.

5. Place 2 rows of peas and raisins (rotten teeth) between each set of lips. Arrange on a serving platter, pucker up, and dig in!

Serves 4 to 6 cavity-prone crones.

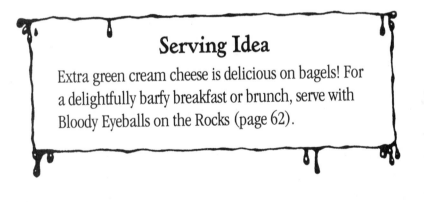

Serving Idea

Extra green cream cheese is delicious on bagels! For a delightfully barfy breakfast or brunch, serve with Bloody Eyeballs on the Rocks (page 62).

Strained Eye Balls

Fresh from the optometrist's garbage to your kitchen table!

6 eggs
1 (6-ounce) tub whipped cream cheese
1 (7-ounce) jar green olives with pimientos
red food coloring

What You'll Need
medium-sized saucepan • sharp knife
• teaspoon • toothpick

1. Place the eggs in a saucepan and cover them with cold water. With an adult's help, cook over high heat until the water begins to boil. Then turn the heat to low and simmer (low boil) for 10 minutes.

2. Place the cooked eggs in cold water. When they're cool enough to touch, crack the eggshells all over by rolling them on a hard surface. Peel away the shells carefully and cut the eggs in half widthwise. (See illustration.)

3. Remove the yolks from the eggs and fill the empty yolk holes with cream cheese. (You won't need the yolks for this recipe.)

4. Press an olive into each cream cheese eyeball, pimiento facing up, for an eerie green iris and startling red pupil!

5. For a final touch, dip the tip of a toothpick in red food coloring and draw broken blood vessels in the cream cheese. Your guests' eyes will pop when they spot these creepy peepers!

Serves 6 eyeball eaters.

Serving Idea

Have guests draw scary monster faces on paper plates (using nontoxic crayons!), leaving *out* the eyes. Slip a pair of Strained Eye Balls in their place and serve.

Ear Wax Wieners on Cotton Swabs

Don't wash behind your ears! Harvest that wax for your next party!

8 tablespoons (1 stick) butter or margarine, melted
24 cocktail franks
½ cup mustard
½ cup mayonnaise

What You'll Need
small pan • broiling pan • basting brush • small mixing bowl
• long-handled fork or spatula • serving platter
• toothpicks • cotton balls

1. With an adult's help, melt the butter or margarine in a small pan over low heat, being careful not to burn it.

2. Place the franks on a broiling pan and carefully brush them with melted butter.

3. With an adult's help, broil the franks until they are evenly browned. (Have an adult turn the franks 2 or 3 times while they are broiling.)

4. While the franks are cooking, combine the mustard and mayonnaise in a small bowl and set aside. This will be your ear wax.

18

5. Arrange the cooked franks on a serving platter.

6. Pierce each frank with a toothpick, then stick a wet cotton ball on the end of each pick. Place the small bowl of ear wax in the middle of the platter, surrounded by franks. You're ready to swab and eat!

Serves 4 to 6 ear pickers.

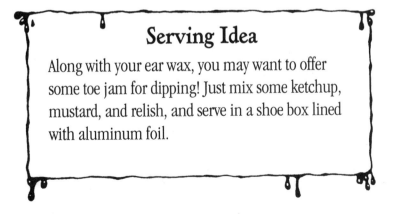

Serving Idea

Along with your ear wax, you may want to offer some toe jam for dipping! Just mix some ketchup, mustard, and relish, and serve in a shoe box lined with aluminum foil.

Pus Pockets

They're delightful when squeezed!

4 small pita breads
2 cups mozzarella cheese, shredded (½ pound)
ketchup

What You'll Need
sharp knife • teaspoon • ungreased cookie sheet • serving platter

1. With an adult's help, preheat the oven to 350 degrees.

2. Slit open each pita bread along ¼ of its edge to make a pocket, and spoon ½ cup of shredded cheese into each one.

3. Place the stuffed pitas on an ungreased cookie sheet.

4. Bake for 15 minutes, or until the pitas turn golden brown. Remove from the oven.

5. With a knife, poke a hole in the top of each pita. *Carefully* squeeze pitas (they'll be hot!) until a little melted cheese oozes out of the hole. Dab ketchup around the hole and arrange on a platter. Now you can not only pick your pimples, but you can eat them, too!

Serves 4 pimple poppers.

Slimy Soups
and Scary Salads

Witch's Brew

Bubble, bubble, toil and trouble . . .

6 chicken wings (buzzard wings)
6 lamb riblets (squirrel legs)
4 chicken necks (severed necks)
½ teaspoon salt
½ teaspoon pepper
2 (10¾-ounce) cans tomato soup
2 cups water
2-4 fresh basil leaves (or ½ teaspoon dried basil)

What You'll Need
2 large pots • long-handled stirring spoon
• slotted spoon • ladle • soup bowls

1. Rinse the meat, or body parts, and place them in a large pot with enough water to cover the meat. Add the salt and pepper and, with an adult's help, cook over medium heat until the water comes to a boil. Lower the heat and continue to simmer, uncovered, for about 45 to 60 minutes, or until the meat is thoroughly cooked.

2. While the meat is cooking, mix the 2 cans of tomato soup and 2 cups of water in another large pot. Stir in the basil and cook over medium heat until your brew begins to boil. Turn the heat to low and simmer, uncovered, for 15 minutes, continuously stirring with a long spoon.

3. When the meat is fully cooked, ask an adult to carefully transfer it with a slotted spoon into the soup mixture.

4. Ladle brew into individual bowls.

Serves 6 witches and/or warlocks.

Serving Idea

As your guests slurp down this delightful dish, be sure to point out when they're gnawing on a buzzard wing, severed neck, or squirrel leg! And don't neglect to remind them not to swallow any bones! Cackle! Cackle!

Bleeding Gums Gumbo

Your dentist's worst nightmare comes true!

2 fresh tomatoes
2 sweet red bell peppers, cores
  and seeds removed
1 (10¾-ounce) can chicken
  gumbo soup

1 (10¾-ounce) can tomato soup
2 cups water
1 (11-ounce) can corn kernels,
  drained

What You'll Need
sharp knife • large saucepan • mixing spoon
• soup ladle • soup bowls

1. With an adult's help, carefully chop tomatoes into small blood-clotty pieces and red peppers into gum shapes. (See illustration.) Set aside.

2. Pour the soups and water into a large saucepan and, with an adult's help, cook at medium heat until the mixture comes to a boil. Lower the heat and let simmer.

3. Add the blood clots, gums, and corn kernels (rotting teeth) to the soup and continue to simmer, stirring occasionally, for about 5 minutes (or until gums are tender). Ladle into individual soup bowls.

Serves 8 dental patients in need of a checkup.

Serving Idea
Chew a plaque-disclosing tablet before serving soup!

Varicose Veins on a Leaf

*So you think blood tastes good? Try eating the veins
that blood runs through!*

1 (15½-ounce) can French-cut string beans, undrained
1 head iceberg lettuce
red food coloring
6 tablespoons sliced almonds

What You'll Need
medium-sized saucepan • serving platter
• glass bowl • slotted spoon

1. With an adult's help, heat the beans in their liquid according to directions on the can.

2. Wash and dry the lettuce and arrange the leaves on a serving platter.

3. Pour the beans and liquid into a glass bowl. Add red food coloring, drop by drop, until the liquid turns the color of blood.

4. Place the bowl in the refrigerator for 15 minutes.

5. Using a slotted spoon, remove the veins and place them in a veinlike pattern on top of each other on the lettuce leaves. (See illustration.)

6. Sprinkle almonds over the beans for an added bony crunch and flavor.

Serves 4 deviant diners.

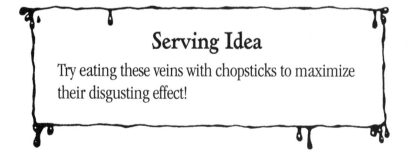

Serving Idea

Try eating these veins with chopsticks to maximize their disgusting effect!

Toxic Tomatoes

WARNING! THIS DISH CONTAINS INGREDIENTS HAZARDOUS TO YOUR MENTAL HEALTH!

6 medium-sized tomatoes
½ avocado, peeled, pitted, and chopped
1 cup grated Swiss cheese (¼ pound)
6–10 chopped fresh basil leaves (or 1 tablespoon dried basil)
¼ teaspoon dried oregano

What You'll Need
sharp knife • cookie sheet • small mixing bowl
• mixing spoon • broiling pan

1. Wash the tomatoes and cut them in half crosswise. Place the halves—open side up—on a cookie sheet.

2. In a small bowl, mash together the avocado (sludge), grated Swiss cheese (pus), and basil (poisonous plant matter). Spoon the mixture on top of the tomatoes and sprinkle with oregano (fly wings). (See illustration.)

3. With an adult's help, broil the tomatoes for 5 minutes or until pus begins to ooze.

4. Carefully remove the tomatoes from the broiler and serve hot.

Serves 4 to 6 madcap mutants.

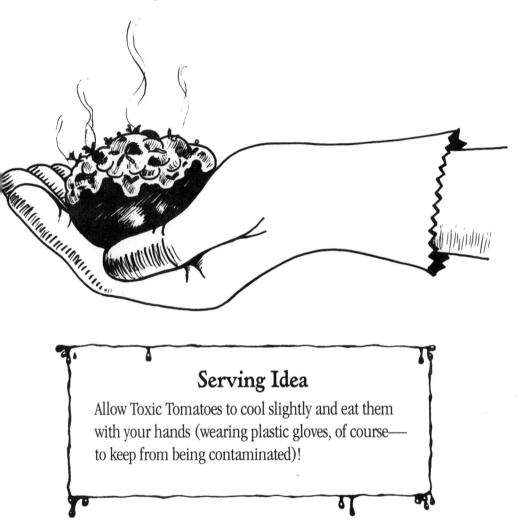

Serving Idea

Allow Toxic Tomatoes to cool slightly and eat them with your hands (wearing plastic gloves, of course—to keep from being contaminated)!

Werewolf in the Waldorf Salad

A "formal" first course that will make your guests howl!

2 large apples
1 tablespoon lemon juice
½ cup golden raisins
½ cup chopped walnuts
1 cup diced celery
½ cup mayonnaise
½ tablespoon milk
1 teaspoon sugar

½ head iceberg lettuce
8 leaves of endive or other curly,
   leafy greens
a large handful of alfalfa sprouts
4 carrots, peeled and sliced
   lengthwise into 2-inch pieces
4 radishes

What You'll Need
sharp knife • large bowl • small bowl
• mixing spoon • salad plates

1. With an adult's help, peel, core, and dice the apples. Toss the diced apples in a large bowl with the lemon juice. (The lemon juice will keep them from turning brown.)

2. Add the raisins, nuts, and celery to the apple pieces and toss together.

3. In a small bowl, mix the mayonnaise, milk, and sugar until well blended. This mixture is your dressing.

4. Add the dressing to the ingredients in the large bowl and toss. This is your Waldorf Salad.

5. Place 2 or 3 lettuce leaves on individual salad plates and spoon the Waldorf Salad over the lettuce in a "head" shape. To create the werewolf in your Waldorf, decorate each salad with pointy endive ears, alfalfa-sprout hair and beard, pointy carrot fangs, and radish-half eyeballs.

Serves 4 humans (or 1 hungry werewolf).

Serving Idea

Try serving this salad on the night of a full moon (the time when people traditionally turn into werewolves). After dinner, pop a werewolf movie into your VCR!

Fungus Among Us
Vegetable Salad

Why use a friend's fungus when you can grow your own?

1 (9-ounce) package frozen creamed spinach	2 cucumbers
½ head iceberg lettuce	2 tomatoes
4 carrots	6-8 radishes
	2 red onions

What You'll Need
saucepan • paper towels • large salad bowl
• vegetable peeler • sharp knife

1. Prepare the creamed spinach in the saucepan according to the directions on the package and let it cool in the refrigerator for 30 minutes.

2. Wash the lettuce, carrots, cucumbers, tomatoes, and radishes in cold water. Pat the lettuce dry with paper towels, tear it into small pieces, and place it in a salad bowl.

3. With an adult's help, peel the carrots, cucumbers, and onions, then slice all the vegetables into small pieces. Add to the salad bowl.

4. Pour the cooled creamed spinach (fungus) into the salad bowl and toss.

Serves 6 to 8 fun guys.

Main Corpses

Gnarled Witch's Fingers

May we "point" out that these fingers have a special, crunchy bite?

1 tablespoon vegetable oil
4 chicken cutlets
1 cup all-purpose flour
1 egg, beaten
1 cup seasoned breadcrumbs

1 (6-ounce) can black olives, drained
1 head iceberg lettuce, shredded

What You'll Need
cookie sheet • sharp knife or scissors
• 3 soup bowls • serving platter

1. Grease a cookie sheet with vegetable oil and set aside.

2. With an adult's help, carefully slice the cutlets with a knife or clean scissors into strips about the width of 1 finger. Do not cut them perfectly straight—the more crooked, the better.

3. Put the flour, egg, and breadcrumbs into separate soup bowls and line the bowls up next to each other.

4. Dust the chicken strips with flour, working with 2 or 3 at a time. Then dip them into the bowl of beaten egg.

5. Roll each strip in breadcrumbs. Place strips on the greased cookie sheet.

6. With an adult's help, broil Witch's Fingers for 5 minutes on each side, or until they are golden brown.

7. To make fingernails, cut the olives in half lengthwise. Trim the halves into pointy nail shapes as shown.

8. Carefully place olives on hot Witch's Finger "tips" and arrange on a shredded head (of lettuce, of course!).

Serves 4 wittle witches.

Serving Idea

If you prefer your fingers more moist, try dipping them in barbecue sauce (coagulated blood sauce) or honey mustard salad dressing (for a painfully pus-covered look). Bone appétit!

Frank-in-Steins

Why have a cup of soup when you can have a stein of franks?

1 (16-ounce) package hot dogs   mustard
1 (16-ounce) can sauerkraut   ketchup

What You'll Need
beer steins or coffee mugs • long-handled fork • sharp knife

1. With an adult's help, prepare the hot dogs and sauerkraut according to directions on the packages.

2. With a long-handled fork, divide the sauerkraut equally among the steins, filling each no more than half full.

3. Carefully cut the cooked hot dogs into small pieces and drop into steins. Allow guests to dribble mustard (yellow pus) or ketchup (thickened blood) over their Frank-in-Steins.

Serves 8 monsters.

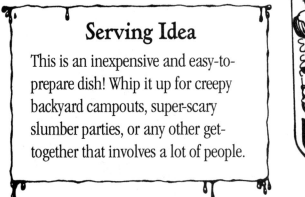

Serving Idea

This is an inexpensive and easy-to-prepare dish! Whip it up for creepy backyard campouts, super-scary slumber parties, or any other get-together that involves a lot of people.

Tongues on Toast

Now here's a dish that will get your friends' tongues wagging.

8 slices white bread   mustard
8 slices bologna

What You'll Need
scissors • dull knife • serving platter

1. With clean scissors, cut each slice of bread into a closed mouth shape. Then, with a dull knife, cut an opening between the upper and lower lips. (See illustration.)

2. With an adult's help, cut the bologna with scissors into thin, tonguelike strips. (You can eat the unused parts!) Place the tongues between the bread lips so that the tongues hang out of the mouths.

3. Spread mustard on the bread and toast lightly in a toaster oven or under the broiler until the bread is golden brown. Once cooked, arrange on a serving platter—and try not to talk with your mouth full!

Serves 4 blabbermouths.

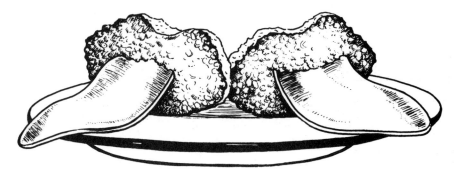

Dead Man's Meat Loaf

Did the butler do it, or the cow?

1½ pounds ground beef
1 egg, beaten
1 cup breadcrumbs
1 tablespoon ketchup
1 teaspoon salt
¼ teaspoon garlic powder

¼ teaspoon pepper
¼ cup minced onion
1 large (26-ounce) jar spaghetti
  sauce
olives, corn kernels, and
  pimientos for garnish

What You'll Need
large mixing bowl • baking pan

1. With an adult's help, preheat the oven to 350 degrees.

2. Using clean hands, mix together all the ingredients (except for spaghetti sauce and garnishes) in a large bowl.

3. To form the corpse: In an ungreased baking pan, sculpt the meat mixture into a body. (Generally, bodies have a single head, torso, 2 legs, and 2 arms, but yours can have as many or few as you like.)

4. Using olives for eyes, corn kernels for teeth, and pimientos for a tongue, decorate your loaf. (Feel free to try other vegetables, too. For example, carrot coins and peas work nicely as eyes and buttons.)

5. Pour spaghetti sauce around the corpse and, with an adult's help, bake for approximately 1 hour and 15 minutes. (Your oven may cook at a different rate, so have an adult make sure the meat is fully cooked before removing the loaf from the oven.)

Serves 6 creepy carnivores.

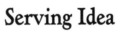

Serving Idea

Right before serving, stick a dagger (or butter knife) into the "heart" of the corpse as a garnish.

Brains on the Half Skull

You don't have to be a genius to enjoy this dish!

2 medium-sized potatoes
1 (8-ounce) package thin spaghetti
1 (14-ounce) jar spaghetti sauce

What You'll Need
sharp knife • baking pan • medium-sized pot • colander • small pot
• mixing bowl • tablespoon • oven mitts

1. With an adult's help, preheat the oven to 400 degrees.

2. Wash the potatoes and cut them in half crosswise. (See illustration.) Place the potatoes cut side up on a baking pan and bake for 40 minutes.

3. While the potatoes bake, prepare the spaghetti in a medium-sized pot according to the directions on the package. Then, with an adult's help, carefully drain the cooked spaghetti in a colander over the sink.

4. A few minutes before the potatoes are ready, begin to heat the spaghetti sauce (blood) in a small pot.

5. With an adult's help, remove the potatoes from the oven. Then, wearing oven mitts, scoop out the insides of the potatoes. (You won't need the insides for this recipe.) The empty shells will serve as skulls.

6. When the sauce begins to boil, remove it from the heat and combine it with the cooked spaghetti to make brains. Put a scoop of bloody brains in each skull, take off your thinking cap, and enjoy!

Serves 4 brainiacs.

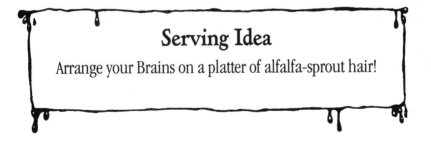

Serving Idea

Arrange your Brains on a platter of alfalfa-sprout hair!

Gangrenous
Scrambled Legs

You won't get sick eating these eggs—but you may turn green!

1 dozen small sausage links
8 eggs
8 tablespoons milk
1 teaspoon salt
¼ teaspoon pepper

green food coloring
1-2 tablespoons butter or
   margarine
¼ cup chopped onions

What You'll Need
sharp knife • aluminum foil • medium-sized mixing bowl
• wire whisk or eggbeater • large frying pan
• long-handled fork or spatula • serving platter or plates

1. With an adult's help, prepare the sausage links according to the directions on the package. After they have cooled slightly, carefully slice them in half lengthwise. Wrap them in aluminum foil and set aside.

2. In a medium-sized mixing bowl, combine the eggs, milk, salt, and pepper. Beat with a whisk until frothy. Slowly add food coloring, 1 drop at a time, until you reach your desired shade of gangrene green.

3. With an adult's help, heat a tablespoon of butter or margarine in a large frying pan over medium heat until the butter begins to sizzle. Add the chopped onions (toenails) and sauté for a few minutes. Then add the egg mixture to the pan.

42

4. Stir the egg mixture with a long-handled fork or spatula until the eggs are firm and not too runny. When the eggs are almost done, add the sausage links (little legs) and cook just until the sausage is heated.

5. Transfer the Gangrenous Scrambled Legs to individual plates or a serving platter.

Serves 4 barfing breakfasters.

Serving Idea

You can sprinkle shredded mozzarella cheese on top of hot, just-cooked eggs and—voilà!—in just a minute your Gangrenous Scrambled Legs are nice and pus-covered.

Spaghetti and Eyeballs

You'll see, this tastes great (and looks gross)!

1½ pounds ground beef
1 cup seasoned breadcrumbs
1 tablespoon ketchup
1 egg
¼ teaspoon pepper
½ teaspoon oregano

1 (7-ounce) jar pimiento-stuffed
  olives
1 (14-ounce) jar spaghetti sauce
3 quarts water
1 teaspoon salt
1 (8-ounce) package spaghetti
2 tablespoons butter or margarine

What You'll Need
large mixing bowl • mixing spoon • baking dish • large pot
• colander • serving bowl • serving spoon

1. With an adult's help, preheat the oven to 350 degrees.

2. Mix the ground beef, breadcrumbs, ketchup, egg, pepper, and oregano in a large bowl. Then form the meat mixture into about 18 to 24 eyeball-sized balls. (See illustration.)

3. Press an olive into each eyeball, pimiento side out. Place the eyeballs in a baking dish, cover them with the spaghetti sauce, and, with an adult's help, bake for 45 minutes.

4. About 15 minutes before the eyeballs are done, fill a large pot with 3 quarts of water. Add salt. With an adult's help, set on medium heat and follow package directions to cook the spaghetti.

5. After the spaghetti has cooked, ask an adult to carefully drain it in a colander over the sink. Transfer it to a serving bowl and toss with the butter or margarine (so the spaghetti doesn't stick together).

6. When your eyeballs are done, carefully remove them from the oven and spoon onto the spaghetti, irises up. Spoon sauce from the pan around them.

Serves 6 evil optometrists.

Serving Idea

Slice pitted black olives into thin slivers. Label them "eyelashes" and serve with your Spaghetti and Eyeballs!

Worms au Gratin

A dish that will burrow its way into your heart!

To make worms
4 quarts water
1 tablespoon salt
2 cups (6-7 ounces) egg noodles
2 cups (8 ounces) spaghetti, broken into short pieces
2 tablespoons butter or margarine
1½ cups grated American cheese
½ teaspoon vegetable oil

To make dirt
2 slices whole-wheat bread, toasted
1 tablespoon butter or margarine, melted
¼ teaspoon salt

What You'll Need
large pot • colander • large bowl • mixing spoon
• casserole dish • small bowl

1. To prepare the worms: Fill a large pot with 4 quarts of water and add the salt. With an adult's help, heat over medium to high heat until the water comes to a rapid boil.

2. Carefully add the egg noodles and spaghetti (worms) and allow the water to come to a boil again. Lower the heat and cook the worms on a slow boil, uncovered, for about 8 to 10 minutes.

3. Ask an adult to carefully drain the worms through a colander and pour them into a large bowl. Toss with butter or margarine and the grated cheese.

46

4. Grease the inside of a casserole dish with the vegetable oil. Pour the cooked worms into the dish and set aside.

5. To prepare the dirt: In a small bowl, crumble the whole-wheat toast into tiny crumbs. (The more well-toasted the bread is, the easier it will be to create crumbs.)

6. Mix melted butter and salt with the crumbs to create dirt.

7. Sprinkle dirt over worms and, with an adult's help, place the casserole under the broiler for 5 minutes. Then make like an invertebrate and dig in!

Serves 6 ghouls or boils.

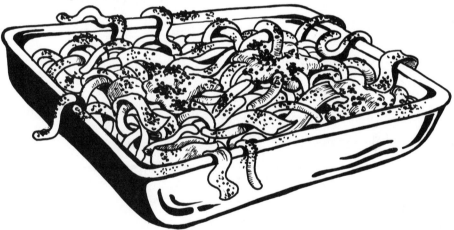

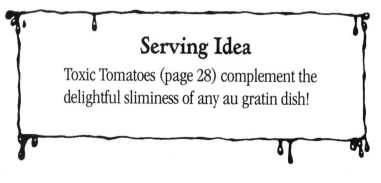

Serving Idea

Toxic Tomatoes (page 28) complement the delightful sliminess of any au gratin dish!

Chips and Lips

Pucker up for a lip-smacking treat!

6 English muffins
2 cups shredded mozzarella cheese (½ pound)
6 medium-sized tomatoes

What You'll Need
ungreased cookie sheet • knife • teaspoon • scissors

1. Separate English muffins into halves. Arrange halves on a cookie sheet, rough side up.

2. Place a layer of shredded mozzarella cheese on each muffin half.

3. Cut the tomatoes in half and use a teaspoon to scoop out the tomato pulp. Use a knife or a pair of clean scissors to cut out the outlines of pairs of lips from the tomato skins. (See illustration.)

4. Place a pair of lips, shiny side up, on each muffin half. Then, with an adult's help, place the cookie sheet under the broiler for 3 to 5 minutes, or until the cheese begins to brown.

5. Carefully remove the cookie sheet from the broiler and place 1 or 2 muffin halves on each plate. Try not to drool as you offer up this lip-smacking snack to your hungry guests!

Serves 6 to 8 fiendish friends.

Serving Idea

To round out your meal, add some tasty skin peelings (potato chips), and drizzle lightly with ketchup blood! Or add some onion fangs to give them a real bite!

Chuckie's Upchuck

Uh-oh, Chuckie's back, and he's brought up something special for dinner!

2 teaspoons butter or margarine
2 medium-sized onions, chopped
2 (8-ounce) cans cream-style corn
2 (10¾-ounce) cans cream of mushroom soup
2 cups milk
tomatoes, leftover green beans, mushrooms (or whatever other vegetables you have in your refrigerator)

What You'll Need
large saucepan • long-handled spoon or spatula
• knife • soup ladle • serving bowls

1. With an adult's help, melt the butter in a large saucepan over low heat. Add the chopped onions and sauté until they are softened and light brown.

2. Add the corn, soup, and milk to the onions and stir together.

3. With an adult's help, cut up all the vegetables you will be using into small pieces. Add them to the saucepan and cook over medium heat until the upchuck begins to boil. Turn down the heat immediately and continue cooking on low for about 5 minutes.

4. Ladle the upchuck into individual bowls. (Chuckie wants you to remember *his* upchuck makes a delicious vegetarian meal.)

Serves 6 sickies.

Serving Idea

Be prepared for accidental messes! Place a brown paper lunch bag on your dinner table, write "BARF BAG" on the front of it with a marker, and fill it with extra paper napkins. You can't be too safe when Chuckie's Upchuck is on the table!

Slash 'Em, Gash 'Em Spuds

Even your best friends can be psycho-slashers!

6 medium-sized russet potatoes
2 teaspoons salt
½ cup milk
4 tablespoons (½ stick) butter or margarine, softened
1 teaspoon pepper
8-12 small mushrooms
2 sweet red bell peppers, cored, seeded, and sliced
assorted vegetables (broccoli, zucchini, carrots, etc.)
ketchup
additional melted butter

What You'll Need
vegetable peeler • sharp knife • large pot with cover
• slotted spoon • large mixing bowl • electric mixer
• salad plates • blunt knife

1. With an adult's help, carefully peel off potato skins with a vegetable peeler.

2. Cut potatoes into quarters and put them in a large pot ¾ full of cold water. Add 1 teaspoon of salt to the water, cover the pot, and, with an adult's help, boil for 15 to 20 minutes, or until the potatoes are soft.

3. Using a slotted spoon, carefully remove potatoes from the hot water and place in a large mixing bowl. Add the milk, butter, pepper, and the remaining 1 teaspoon of salt. With an adult's help, beat with an electric mixer for 3 to 4 minutes, or until light and fluffy.

52

4. Spoon a mound of potatoes onto individual salad plates. Allow to cool slightly, then, using clean hands, sculpt a human head on each plate.

5. Using vegetables of your choice, add eyes, a nose, and a mouth to each head. (Try mushrooms for eyes, red pepper slices for lips, broccoli for hair or mustaches, etc.)

6. Using a blunt knife, slash a gash down the side of each head. Pour ketchup (blood) into each gash and dribble on melted-butter pus for a deliciously disgusting side dish!

Serves 4 to 6 slasher-ettes.

Serving Idea

Serve Slash 'Em, Gash 'Em Spuds ungarnished and let your guests dress and slash 'em. Then give a hand (made out of potatoes, of course) to the maker of the best one!

Wild Lice

At last! A delicious use for pesky parasites!

2 cups orzo (rice-shaped pasta)
¼ cup light cream
2 tablespoons butter
¾ cup grated Parmesan cheese
1 tablespoon chopped fresh parsley
   (or 1 teaspoon dried parsley)

½ teaspoon pepper
½ teaspoon vegetable oil
1 ham steak, approximately
   1½ pounds

What You'll Need
large cooking pot • colander • large mixing bowl • casserole dish

1. With an adult's help, preheat the oven to 350 degrees.

2. Prepare the orzo according to the directions on the package.

3. With an adult's help, carefully drain the orzo through a colander over the sink. Pour the orzo into a large bowl and add to it the cream, butter, cheese, parsley, and pepper. Toss well.

4. Grease a casserole dish with the vegetable oil. Place the ham steak in the dish and then cover it with orzo (lice). With an adult's help, bake for 20 to 30 minutes.

Serves 8 little
buggers.

Putrid Potions

Mucous Membrane Milkshake

Mmm, mmm, mmm! Mucus makes a creamy treat!

2 cups buttermilk
2 scoops vanilla ice cream
½ cup pineapple juice

4 tablespoons brown sugar
2 cups milk

What You'll Need
blender • tall glasses • small pan • wooden spoon

1. Measure all the ingredients except the milk into a blender. Then, with an adult's help, blend on medium speed until smooth and creamy. (Add more ice cream if you like your mucus extra thick.)

2. Fill the tall glasses with the mixture and refrigerate.

3. With an adult's help, heat the milk in a small pan over medium heat until it begins to boil. Remove from the heat and let it cool until a film develops on its surface. Using a wooden spoon, carefully scoop off the film and place some on top of each milkshake.

4. If you need more mucus, just reheat the remaining milk and repeat this step. Be careful not to burn the milk or your Mucous Membrane Milkshake will taste disgusting instead of delicious!

Serves 4 phlegm fanciers.

Serving Idea

Blend chunks of pineapple into your milkshake (for phlegm balls) or red cherries (for blood clots)!

Ghoul-ade over Gopher Guts

You'll go nuts over these slimy guts!

1 (3-ounce) package cherry or strawberry gelatin dessert
  mix (such as Jell-O)
10-12 lemons (or 2 cups bottled lemon juice)
7 cups water
1 cup sugar
green food coloring

What You'll Need
small mixing bowl • pitcher • long-handled spoon • glasses

1. With an adult's help, prepare a bowl of gelatin dessert according to the directions on the package. Chill in the freezer for 45 minutes or until *partially* set.

2. While the gelatin cools, squeeze the juice from the lemons into a pitcher. Be careful not to include any seeds! (Bottled lemon juice can be substituted for fresh lemon juice.)

3. Add the 7 cups of water to the lemon juice. Stir. Add the sugar and stir again.

4. Add green food coloring until Ghoul-ade is the desired shade.

5. 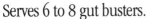 Pour Ghoul-ade into individual drinking glasses, then spoon partially set gelatin gopher guts into glasses. Raise a glass and make a ghoul-icious toast!

Serves 6 to 8 gut busters.

Serving Idea

Include long spoons when serving this drink, to help your guests eat their guts out!

Bloody Bug Juice

Comatose creatures make this zesty drink delicious!

2 (12-ounce) packages frozen
   strawberries, defrosted
1 (6-ounce) can lemonade
   concentrate, thawed

1 quart ginger ale
1 cup raisins
1 cup blueberries, fresh or
   frozen

What You'll Need
bowl • fork • pitcher • tall glasses

1. Place the strawberries in a bowl and mash with a fork.

2. In a large pitcher, mix the strawberry mash, lemonade, and ginger ale.

3. Place handfuls of raisins and blueberries (bugs) into tall glasses. Pour the liquid over the bugs, then sit back and watch the bugs and scum rise to the top of each glass!

Serves 6 little bloodsuckers.

Serving Idea

To quench a creepy crowd's thirst, double or triple this recipe and serve in a punch bowl. Drape some gummy worms over the rim of your bowl for a particularly swampy-looking effect!

Sulfuric Acid Swig

Don't throw this *drink in anyone's face!*

1 (6-ounce) can lemonade
concentrate, partially defrosted
½ cup lemon juice

1 cup cold grapefruit juice
2 quarts lemon sherbet
1 quart cold club soda

What You'll Need
large pitcher • long-handled spoon • tall glasses • ice-cream scoop

1. In a large pitcher, mix together the lemonade concentrate, lemon juice, and grapefruit juice. Add to this the amount of water required on the lemonade can.

2. Pour the liquid into tall glasses, filling them halfway, and add a scoop of lemon sherbet to each.

3. Fill the glasses with club soda, pucker up, and serve immediately.

Serves 8 to 10 mad scientists.

Serving Idea

Just before serving, sprinkle the top of each glass with a pinch of lemon- or lime-flavored powdered drink mix. Makes for a totally toxic-looking treat!

Bloody Eyeballs
on the Rocks

You can "see" this drink is eye-deal on a hot day!

12 radishes
1 (7-ounce) jar pimiento-stuffed olives
1 (46-ounce) can tomato juice

What You'll Need
vegetable peeler • ice cube tray • tall glasses

1. Prepare these bloody eyeballs the day before you plan to serve them. With an adult's help, peel 12 radishes, leaving thin streaks of red skin on them for blood vessels.

2. Using the tip of the vegetable peeler or a small knife, carefully scoop out a small hole in each radish. Stuff a green olive, pimiento side out, in each hole. Place 1 radish eyeball in each section of an empty ice cube tray. (You may need to pare your eyeballs down a bit to fit in the ice cube tray.)

3. Fill the tray with water and freeze overnight.

4. Pour tall glasses ¾ full of tomato juice and add a pair of eyeballs to each glass. Cheers! This blood's for you!

Serves 6 thirsty creeps.

Dead-zerts and Sickening Snacks

Viennese Vampire Fangs

The sweeter the blood, the happier the vampire!

4-6 large apples
¼ cup bottled lemon juice
½ cup sugar

1 (10-ounce) jar strawberry fruit
sauce or "all fruit" preserves

What You'll Need
vegetable peeler • sharp knife • mixing bowl
• wooden spoon • party platter

1. With an adult's help, carefully peel the apples, core them, and cut them in half. Then cut each apple in half again to make quarters. Cut each quarter again to make eighths. (See illustration.)

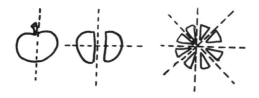

2. Place the cut apples in a bowl and toss with the lemon juice. (This will keep them from turning brown.)

3. To prepare fangs, cut and shape the apple eighths as shown in the illustration. When the fangs are cut, return them to the bowl with the lemon juice and toss lightly.

4. Sprinkle sugar over the fangs and toss until evenly mixed throughout.

5. Arrange the fangs on a party platter splattered with strawberry sauce blood. Take a bite, my sweet!

Serves 4 to 6 Viennese vampires.

Serving Idea

Vampires love to dress for dinner, so be sure to dust talcum powder on your face and color your lips with red lipstick when serving this dish. Don't forget to dim the lights!

Raisin Gnats

If something's bugging you, it helps to have a tasty snack.

1 (8-ounce) package semisweet chocolate chips
1 (9-ounce) box raisins
1 small package shredded coconut
1 (6-ounce) package lime gelatin dessert mix (such as Jell-O)

What You'll Need
large pot • small pot • wooden stirring spoon • table fork
• cookie sheet • waxed paper • dessert bowls

1. With an adult's help, prepare a double boiler to melt chocolate in. Heat 2 inches of water to simmering (not boiling) in the bottom part of the double boiler.

2. Place the chocolate chips in the top of the double boiler. Set the top into the bottom part and melt over low heat. Once the chocolate begins to melt, stir constantly until it is fully melted. Remove from the heat and set aside to cool for about 5 minutes.

3. To prepare gnats, spear raisins on each tine of a table fork. Dip the fork into the melted chocolate, and then arrange the raisins on a cookie sheet covered with waxed paper. Repeat until all the raisins are chocolate-covered. Stick 2 pieces of shredded coconut antennae onto each raisin and freeze for 20 to 30 minutes.

4. With an adult's help, prepare gelatin dessert according to the directions on the package. Pour into individual dessert bowls and set in the freezer for 20 minutes or until the gelatin begins to harden.

5. Remove the gelatin when it's partially set (it should be a little firm to the touch) and arrange gnats on top of the gelatin.

6. Refrigerate until the gelatin sets completely.

Serves 4 to 6 big buggers.

Serving Idea

To prepare Raisin Gnats for a big, buggy group, follow the above directions, but use a gelatin mold instead of individual dessert bowls. When you are ready to serve dessert, ask an adult to help you dip the mold in warm water and loosen the edge of the gelatin with a blunt knife. Place a dinner plate face down on top of the mold, hold the 2 together tightly, and flip them over. Gently shake and lift off mold. Your friends will shake with delight at seeing this jiggly dead-zert!

Ghosts on Broomsticks

Is it a bird, a plane, or a spooky Halloween treat?

1 pound white chocolate chips
½ cup tiny red cinnamon candies

What You'll Need
large pot • small pot • wooden spoon • 2 cookie sheets
• waxed paper • 12 wooden sticks

1. With an adult's help, prepare a double boiler. Heat 2 inches of water to simmering (not boiling) in the larger pot. Place the white chocolate chips in the smaller pot and set it over the pot of simmering water.

2. Cook on low heat, stirring constantly until the chocolate is fully melted. Remove from the heat.

3. Cover 2 cookie sheets with waxed paper. Arrange 12 wooden sticks on the waxed paper, 6 to a sheet.

4. Spoon ghost-shaped blobs of chocolate onto the paper, partially covering each stick. (See illustration.)

5. Press 2 candies into each ghost for eyes.

6. Freeze ghosts for 15 minutes, or until hard.

Makes 12 ghosts.

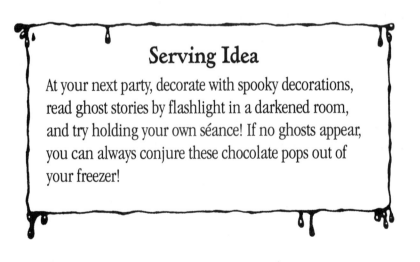

Serving Idea

At your next party, decorate with spooky decorations, read ghost stories by flashlight in a darkened room, and try holding your own séance! If no ghosts appear, you can always conjure these chocolate pops out of your freezer!

Hot Cross Black Widows

The only spiders you can bite back!

To make muffins
1-2 tablespoons butter or
    margarine
1 egg
¼ cup vegetable oil
1 cup milk
2 cups all-purpose flour
3 teaspoons baking powder
1 teaspoon salt
¼ cup granulated sugar

To make frosting
4 ounces cream cheese, softened
3 tablespoons unsalted butter, at
    room temperature
1½ cups confectioners' sugar
½ teaspoon vanilla extract
juice of ¼ lemon (or 1 teaspoon
    bottled lemon juice)
red, green, yellow, and blue food
    coloring
black licorice strings

What You'll Need
muffin pan with 12 muffin cups • fork • large mixing bowl
• wooden spoon • 2 small mixing bowls • baking rack
• electric mixer • rubber spatula • scissors

1. To prepare muffins: With an adult's help, preheat the oven to 400 degrees. Grease the bottoms (but not the sides) of 12 medium-sized muffin cups with the butter or margarine.

2. Beat the egg in a large bowl with a fork. Stir in the vegetable oil and milk.

3. Combine the flour, baking powder, salt, and sugar in a small mixing bowl and stir together. Add to the egg mixture. Stir lightly until the dry ingredients are barely moistened. (The batter should be lumpy.)

4. Fill muffin cups ¾ full of batter. With an adult's help, bake 20 to 30 minutes, or until the muffins turn golden brown. Carefully remove from the oven, turn out of the pan, and set on a rack to cool.

5. To prepare frosting: With an adult's help, mix cream cheese and butter together with an electric mixer. Slowly add confectioners' sugar and continue beating. Add vanilla and lemon juice, and mix thoroughly.

6. Put a small portion of frosting in a separate bowl and mix into it a few drops of red food coloring. Set aside. Color the remaining frosting, drop by drop, with red, green, yellow, and blue food coloring until it is black.

7. With a rubber spatula, spread the black frosting on top of each muffin. Then add a small red Black Widow hourglass to each one. Add legs to your spiders using licorice whip strings. (You may need to cut the licorice into shorter pieces.) Place arachnids on platter and serve!

Makes 12 Hot Cross Black Widows.

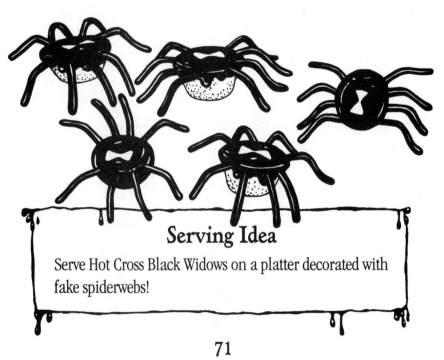

Serving Idea

Serve Hot Cross Black Widows on a platter decorated with fake spiderwebs!

Poached Skull and Crossbones

Little monsters have been known to "lose their heads" over this one.

4 bananas
1 can pear halves, drained
1 handful raisins

strawberry or raspberry fruit sauce,
or "all fruit" preserves

What You'll Need
large baking dish or cookie sheet • blunt knife

1. With an adult's help, preheat the oven to 350 degrees.

2. Cut bananas in half lengthwise and place 2 halves, or bones, crisscrossed in X shapes in a baking dish or on a cookie sheet.

3. Place your pear-half skulls on top of banana X's, curved side up. With a blunt knife, make 2 small slits in the pears for eyes. Insert a raisin in each slit. With an adult's help, bake for 10 to 15 minutes.

4. Remove from the oven and carefully transfer to individual plates. Drip some fruit sauce blood around your creepy crossbones and gobble them in a ghoulish fashion!

Serves 4 little skeletons.

Icky Sticky Sugar Snakes

This slinky dessert has real stick-to-your-ribs flavor!

To make the dough
8 tablespoons (1 stick) unsalted
   butter, at room temperature
3 tablespoons honey
1 teaspoon vanilla extract
1 cup all-purpose flour
½ teaspoon salt
½ teaspoon vegetable oil
½ cup chocolate chips

To make the sticky sauce
½ cup honey
2 tablespoons sugar
2 tablespoons cinnamon

What You'll Need
medium-sized bowl • fork • plastic wrap
• 1 large or 2 small cookie sheets • small bowl • serving platter

1. To prepare dough: With an adult's help, preheat the oven to 300 degrees. In a medium-sized bowl, mash the butter and honey with a fork until blended well.

2. Gradually stir in the vanilla, flour, and salt. (The mixture should have a doughy consistency.)

3. Wrap the dough in plastic wrap and store in the refrigerator for 1 hour. Grease cookie sheets with vegetable oil.

4. After an hour, remove the dough from the refrigerator and separate it into pieces the size of golf balls. (If the dough sticks to your hands, dip them in flour.)

5. Roll out balls between your hands into snakelike shapes, about the length and thickness of your pinky. Separate each ball into 4 smaller sections and roll each section into a snake.

6. Place snakes 1 inch apart on cookie sheets. With an adult's help, bake for 20 to 25 minutes or until snakes begin to turn light brown.

7. Carefully remove the cookie sheets from the oven and immediately remove the snakes from the sheets to a platter. Allow snakes to cool slightly and press 2 chocolate-chip eyes into the head of each snake. Set aside until completely cool.

8. To prepare sticky sauce: Mix honey, sugar, and cinnamon in a small bowl. Drizzle over the cooled snakes and serve.

Makes about 24 Icky Sticky Sugar Snakes.

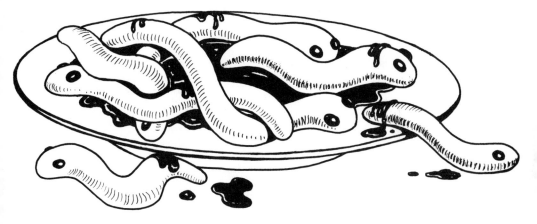

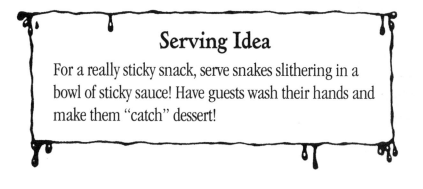

Serving Idea

For a really sticky snack, serve snakes slithering in a bowl of sticky sauce! Have guests wash their hands and make them "catch" dessert!

Tempting Toenail Truffles

Only the finest toenails in the world are used for this tasty, toe-licious treat!

3 ounces semisweet baking chocolate
1 (9-ounce) package pretzel nuggets (bite-sized pretzels)
1 (12-ounce) can beer nuts (sugared peanuts)

What You'll Need
large pot • small pot • long-handled spoon
• small package of toothpicks • waxed paper

1. Carefully remove the thin sugar shells from the beer nuts and put aside.

2. With an adult's help, prepare a double boiler. Heat 2 inches of water to simmering (not boiling) in the larger pot. Place the chocolate in the smaller pot and set it over the simmering water. Stir until the chocolate melts.

3. When the chocolate is melted, remove the small pan from the heat.

Contents

Library of Congress Cataloging-in-Publication Data

Monroe, Lucy.
    Creepy cuisine / by Lucy Monroe; illustrated by Dianne O'Quinn Burke.
      p. cm.
    Summary: A collection of creepy but tasty recipes, including Pus Pockets, Bleeding Gums Gumbo, and Gangrenous Scrambled Legs.
    ISBN 0-679-84402-3 (pbk.)
    1. Halloween cookery—Juvenile literature. [1. Halloween cookery.] I. Burke, Dianne O'Quinn, ill. II. Title.
TX739.2.H34S86 1993
641.5'68—dc20   92-41654

Manufactured in the United States of America

10 9 8 7 6 5 4 3 2

Creepy Cuisine

By Lucy Monroe

Illustrations by Dianne O'Quinn Burke

RANDOM HOUSE   NEW YORK

Phlegm Brûlée

Clear your throat before serving this dish to your most special company!

1 (3-ounce) package lime-flavored gelatin dessert mix
  (such as Jell-O)
2 cups cold milk
1 (3¼-ounce) package instant vanilla pudding

What You'll Need
2 small mixing bowls • 2 mixing spoons
• electric mixer • dessert dishes

1. With an adult's help, prepare lime gelatin dessert according to the directions on the package. Place the bowl of gelatin in the freezer for 40 minutes.

2. While the gelatin is setting in the freezer, pour 2 cups of cold milk into another small bowl and add the pudding mix.

3. With an adult's help, combine the pudding mix and milk with an electric mixer until well blended, about 1 to 2 minutes.

4. Immediately pour the pudding mix into the dessert dishes, leaving room at the top for the phlegm. Let the dishes set in the refrigerator.

4. Carefully insert a toothpick into each pretzel nugget (this seems impossible, but it's not!), then dip the nugget into the melted chocolate. Be sure your pretzel (toe) is completely covered.

5. Place 1 sugar shell (toenail) on the end of each toe. Place on waxed paper to cool and repeat with as many toes as you desire.

Makes 4 to 6 fetid feet.

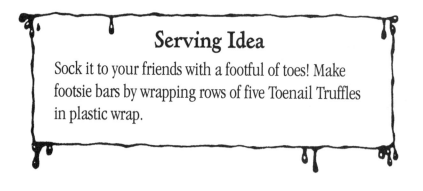

Serving Idea

Sock it to your friends with a footful of toes! Make footsie bars by wrapping rows of five Toenail Truffles in plastic wrap.

5. After the gelatin phlegm firms up to an oozy, semihard state, drizzle over the pudding.

Serves 4 mucus maniacs.

Serving Idea

Garnish with crumpled facial tissues lightly dipped in cold coffee. (The tissues can be tapped lightly with the tip of a red felt pen for a bloody, coughed-up look.) Yum!